Poptropica® English

WORKBOOK 4

Movie Studio Island

T0351908

José Luis Morales • Sagrario Salaberri • Aaron Jolly
Series advisor: David Nunan

Pearson Education Limited
Edinburgh Gate
Harlow
Essex CM20 2JE
England
and Associated Companies throughout the world.

Poptropica English

© Pearson Education Limited 2015

Based on the work of Sagrario Salaberri

The rights of Sagrario Salaberri, Aaron Jolly, and José Luis Morales to be identified as authors of this work have been asserted by them in accordance with the Copyright, Designs and Patents Act 1988.

Phonics syllabus and activities by Rachel Wilson

Editorial and project management by hyphen

All rights reserved; no part of this publication may be reproduced, stored in a retrieval system, or transmitted in any form or by any means, electronic, mechanical, photocopying, recording, or otherwise without the prior written permission of the Publishers.

First published 2015
Twelfth impression 2022

ISBN: 978-1-292-11247-3

Set in Fiendstar 15/24pt

Printed in Slovakia by Neografia

Illustrators: Humberto Blanco (Sylvie Poggio Artists Agency), Anja Boretzki (Good Illustration), Chan Cho Fai, Lee Cosgrove, Leo Cultura, Marek Jagucki, Jim Peacock (Beehive Illustration), Mark Ruffle (The Organisation), and Yam Wai Lun

All other images © Pearson Education Limited

Every effort has been made to trace the copyright holders and we apologize in advance for any unintentional omissions. We would be pleased to insert the appropriate acknowledgement in any subsequent edition of this publication.

Contents

Welcome

1 **Write and match.**

1   He's 10. He has blond hair.
He likes movies. His name is

_____.

2   She's 9. She has black hair.
She loves Finley Keen. Her name is

_____.

3   He has black hair.
He's a movie star. His name is

_____.

4   He has blond hair. He's wearing
a red sweater. His name is

_____.

2 **Draw or stick a picture of yourself and a friend. Then write.**

My name is _____.

I am _____ years old.

I like _____.

My friend's name is _____.

_____ is _____ years old.

_____ likes _____.

Listen and match.

1  Matt

2  Simon

3  Carol

4  Kim

5  Ben

a

b

c

d

e

4 **Write.**

My favorite movie star is _____. _____ can

_____.

5 Write.

smart   shy   quiet   kind   funny

————————

————————

————————

————————

————————

6 Read and match.

1   Alex and Lara are very good friends. They are smart and quiet at school.

2   Alex and Lara help people. They are very kind.

3   They are quiet at school, but they love parties. They are very funny at birthday parties!

7 Circle.

1 A gorilla is (shorter / **taller**) than a giraffe.

2 A hippo is (smaller / **bigger**) than a panda.

3 A mouse is (taller / **smaller**) than a rabbit.

4 A lion is (**faster** / taller) than a horse.

5 A lion is (**bigger** / smaller) than a rabbit.

8 Write.

Billy
12 years old

Andy
7 years old

Sue
9 years old

Darren
11 years old

Jane
10 years old

Christine
8 years old

1 (old / young) Billy is __older than_____ Andy.

2 (old / young) Darren is _____ Billy.

3 (smart / young) Sue is _____ Christine.

4 (smart / young) Jane is _____ Darren.

1 Free time

1 Match.

chatting online

reading magazines

playing the guitar

cooking

watching TV

skiing

playing video games

skateboarding

2 Write.

1 He likes _____.

2 He doesn't like _____.

3 He _____.

4 He _____.

3  **Listen and ✓ = like or ✗ = doesn't like.**

4 **Look at Activity 3 and write.**

1 What does Sophie like doing?

She likes _____ and _____.

She doesn't like _____ and

_____.

2 What does Oliver like doing?

He likes _____ and _____.

He doesn't like _____ and _____.

5 **Write.**

What do you like doing?

I _____.

6 **Listen and write Y = Yes or N = No.**

7 **Look at Activity 6 and write.**

painting   ~~playing hockey~~   riding a scooter   walking the dog

1 Does she like __playing hockey__ ? __Yes__ , she __does__ .

2 Does he like _____ ? _____ , he _____ .

3 Do they like _____ ? _____ , they _____ .

4 Does he like _____ ? _____ , he _____ .

8 **Write about yourself.**

1 Do you like _____ ? _____ , I _____ .

2 Do you like _____ ? _____

3 Do you like _____ ? _____

4 Do you like _____ ? _____

9 Listen and ✓ or ✗.

Me					
My mom					
My dad					

Fiona

10 Look at Activity 9 and write.

1   Does Fiona like playing video games? _Yes, she does._

2   Does Fiona like watching TV? _____

3   What does Fiona's mom like doing? She likes _____.

    She also likes _____ and _____.

4   What does Fiona's dad like doing? He likes _____.

    He also likes _____ and _____.

11 Write questions and answers.

1   Does he like _____?

    _____

2   _____?

    _____

12 **Number the pictures in order.**

13 **Write.**

climbing
faster
jump
riding
skateboarding

1 Coco likes _____ and _____.

2 Sophie loves _____ a scooter.

3 Sophie and Oliver are _____ than Coco.

4 But Coco can _____!

14 **What are Clara's goals? Listen and check (✓).**

1

2

3

4

5

6

15 **Look at Activity 14 and number.**

a   Help people.   ☐

b   Make new friends.   ☐

c   Be a good student.   ☐

d   Be a good son or daughter.   ☐

e   Learn a sport.   ☐

f   Learn to play an instrument.   ☐

16 **Write four goals.**

1   I want to _____.

2   I want to _____.

3   I want to _____.

4   I want to _____.

17 **Listen and read. Then write.**

This is Megan. She lives in a special house. It's a castle. It has 21 rooms and a big yard. She likes playing in the yard and likes reading outside. In the morning she can hear the swans, but at night it's very quiet. She doesn't like cleaning the castle – it's too big!

Name	
House	
Description	
Animals	
Likes	
Doesn't like	

18 **Listen and check (✓).**

1

2

19 **Draw or stick a picture of a special house.**

20 Read the words. Circle the pictures.

blow   cloud   shout   snow

21 Listen and connect the letters. Then write.

1   b   ear   _____

2   ch   ay   _____

3   d   oy   boy

4   y   air   _____

22 Listen and write the words.

1   out   2   _____   3   _____   4   _____

23 Read aloud. Then listen and say.

It's wintertime. The winds blow, and black clouds are low. There is a lot
of snow. Wear a coat, a hat, and a scarf when you go out.

24 Write.

Across →

Down ↓

25 Write.

playing video games ✓
skiing ✓
playing the guitar ✗

reading magazines ✓
riding a scooter ✗
surfing the Internet ✓

1 What does she like doing? She likes _____
_____ and _____ .

2 _____? No, she doesn't.

3 What does he like doing? _____
_____

4 He doesn't _____ .

26 What do or don't you like doing? Check (✓) or X.

1
2
3

4
5
6
7

8
9
10
11

12
13
14
15

27 Look at Activity 26 and write.

I like _____

_____ .

I don't like _____

_____ .

28 Write about your friends or family.

1 My friend likes _____ .

_____ doesn't like _____ .

2 My _____

_____ .

 Are you ready for Unit 2?

2 Wild animals

1 Listen and number.

 a

 b

 c

 d

 e

 f

 g

 h

2 Write.

crocodile   elephant   giraffe   hippo   lion   monkey

 1

 2

 3

It's a lion.

 4

 5

 6

3 What do the animals eat? Write.

fruit   grass   leaves   meat

1   <u>Monkeys eat fruit.</u>   2   _____

3   _____   4   _____

5   _____   6   _____

4 Write.

	Fruit	Leaves	Grass	Meat
Monkeys	✓	✗	✗	✓
Lions	✗	✗	✗	✓
Elephants	✓	✓	✓	✗
Crocodiles	✗	✗	✗	✓

1   Do monkeys eat fruit? _____

2   Do lions eat grass? _____

3   _____ elephants _____ fruit? _____

4   _____ crocodiles _____? _____

5 Match.

1

camel

crab

panda

gorilla

lion

zebra

2

3

4

5

6

6 Unscramble and write. Then number.

1 airn foters ➡ _____

2 lsgasrand ➡ _____

3 tresed ➡ _____

4 evrir ➡ _____

5 oferts ➡ _____

a

b

c

d

e

7 🎧 Listen and write.

1 __Zebras_____ live in _____.

2 _____ live in _____.

3 _____ live in _____.

8 Write.

| big |
| drinking |
| lying |
| walk |

1   _Camels_ eat grass. They don't drink water much. They can run fast, and they can _____ all day.

2   _____ eat fruit and leaves. They like playing with their friends. They are _____ .

3   _____ eat grass and leaves of small trees. They like _____ from the river. They have black and white stripes.

4   _____ eat worms. They like _____ in the mud. They can't run very fast, but they can swim.

9 Look at Activity 8 and write.

1   What do _camels_ eat? They eat _____ .

Where do they live? They live in _____ .

2   What do _____ ? They eat _____ .

Where do _____ ? They live _____ .

3   What _____ ? They _____ .

Where _____ ? They _____ .

4   _____   _____

_____   _____

10 **Number the pictures in order.**

11 **Write.**

1 The animal keeper (knows / doesn't know) where Coco is.

2 The giraffe is eating a (magazine / page from the script).

3 Sophie sees some (bananas / meat) in the rain forest.

4 The gorilla is eating a (banana / page from the script).

5 Uncle James falls into some (paper / fruit) at the end of the story.

12 **Where do the animals live? Write.**

forests   grasslands   rivers

1 Elephants live in _____ and _____.

2 _____ and _____.

3 _____

13 **Write.**

Protect wildlife.

What are they doing to protect wildlife?

He's joining a nature club.   He's learning more about wildlife.

She's recycling.   She's getting her friends to help.

She's giving money.   He's doing a school project.

1

_____

_____

2

_____

_____

3

_____

_____

4

_____

_____

5

_____

_____

6

_____

_____

14 **Look at Activity 13 and choose two things you want to do. Write.**

I want to _____.

I want to _____.

15 **Write.**

1 Elephants live in grasslands and _____.

2 Elephants can _____ more than 300 kg of food a day.

3 Elephants only have four _____.

4 Elephants don't eat _____.

5 Elephants can say _____ with their trunks.

6 Giraffes also live in _____ and forests.

7 Giraffes sometimes eat small _____.

8 Giraffes can live for one _____ without water.

9 Giraffes _____ standing up.

10 Giraffes have long _____ tongues.

16 **Find out about a wild animal. Write.**

An amazing animal	
Name of animal	
They can	
They can't	
They have	
They eat	
They like to	

all   aw

17 Read the words. Circle the pictures.

claw   draw   wall   yawn

18 🎧 Listen and connect the letters. Then write.

1	th	i	n	er	_____
2	d	a	b	er	_____
3	s	u	nn	k	_____
4	c	ow	mm	oy	_____

19 🎧 Listen and write the words.

1 _____   2 _____   3 _____   4 _____

20 🎧 Read aloud. Then listen and say.

Welcome to the zoo. Look at the big cats! They have sharp teeth and sharp claws. I'm glad the wall is tall. You cats can't eat me for dinner!

21 **Write the animals' names. Then match.**

1   **2**    **3**    **4**    **5**

_____   _____   _____   _____   _____

6    **a**    **9**

_____

7    **b**   **10**

_____

          c

8   **d**    **11**

_____   **e**   _____

22 **Write.**

1 Do crocodiles eat fruit? _No,_____. They eat meat.

Where do crocodiles live? _____

2 _____ They eat grass.

Where do zebras live? _____

23 **Draw or stick a picture of an animal. Then write.**

Grassland	River

_____ live in _____.

They eat _____.

They can _____.

They can't _____.

_____ live in _____.

They eat _____.

They can _____.

They can't _____.

Desert	Rain forest

_____

_____

_____

_____

_____

_____

_____

_____

 Are you ready for Unit 3?

3 The seasons

1 Match.

humid

lightning

stormy

thunder

hot

wet

2 Look at Activity 1 and write.

Good day, everybody. What's the weather like today?

Here in the north, it's ^{1} _____. The temperature is

^{2} _____ degrees. Don't forget your hat!

Let's look at the east now. It's ^{3} _____ today.

The temperature is ^{4} _____. Now, let's see the

west. It's ^{5} _____ today. It's cool.

The temperature is ^{6} _____.

In the south the weather is ^{7} _____. There's ^{8} _____

and ^{9} _____. It's ^{10} _____.

3 **Listen and number.**

a □   **b**  □   **c**  □   **d** 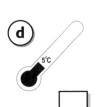 □   **e**  □

4 **Write.**

1 What's the weather like today?

There's _____ and

_____ .

2 What's the weather like today?

It's _____ .

3 What's the weather like today?

It's _____ .

4 What's the weather like today?

It's _____ .

5 What's the temperature today?

It's _____ .

6 What's the temperature today?

It's _____ .

5 Write.

> fall   spring   summer   winter

(1)

It's _____.

(2)

It's _____.

(3)

It's _____.

(4)

It's _____.

6 Write.

> go camping   go hiking   go snowboarding   go water skiing

(1)

_____

(2)

_____

(3)

_____

(4)

_____

7 Look at Activity 6 and write.

1   He goes ___snowboarding___ in the ___winter___.

2   She _____ in the _____.

3   He _____ in the _____.

4   They _____ in the _____.

8 Read and number.

1 She likes eating peaches in the summer.

2 She goes to the park in the winter.

3 She likes watching flowers grow in the spring.

4 She likes flying her kite in the fall.

9 Write.

Hi, Bill! It's hot at the beach. I love going water skiing in the summer.

Hello, Jane! It's cold at the ski slope. I'm wearing my coat and beanie. I love going skiing in the winter.

1 What's the weather like today?

_____

3 What's the temperature today?

_____

5 What does she do in the summer?

_____

2 What's the weather like today?

_____

4 What's the temperature today?

_____

6 What does he do in the winter?

_____

10 Write. Then number the pictures in order.

> Hot milk. Thank you!
> Now there's thunder and lightning!
> We go camping in the summer in this movie.
>
> And now it's snowy and cold!
> It's 38 degrees!
> Where's Sophie?

_____

_____

_____

_____

_____

_____

_____

_____

_____

_____

_____

_____

11 Look at Activity 10 and write.

a What's the temperature? _____

b Does Sophie like milk? _____

c Do they go camping? _____

d Is Sophie a snowman? _____

e Is it snowy and cold? _____

f Is it hot and sunny? _____

12 **Listen and number.**

a

b

c

13 **Write three things a good friend does.**

Cheer your friends up.	Help your friends.
Lie to your friends.	Listen to your friends.
Make fun of your friends.	Talk badly about your friends.

1 _____

2 _____

3 _____

14 **Write about a friend.**

My best friend's name is Karen. We like playing video games together. When Karen is sick or sad, I cheer her up. I give her a card. She likes cards.

_____

_____

_____

_____

15 Circle.

HURRICANE QUIZ

1 The center of the hurricane is
a the heart. **b** the eye.

2 In the center of the hurricane
a it's windy. **b** it isn't windy.

3 There are hurricanes in the
a fall and the summer.
b winter and the spring.

16 Write *hurricane*, *typhoon*, or *cyclone*.

Asia

China _____

Japan _____

North America

USA _____

Mexico _____

Australia

_____

Central America

Cuba _____

Costa Rica _____

17 **Read the words. Circle the pictures.**

chew   fly   new   sky

18 **Listen and connect the letters. Then write.**

1   l   oi   k   _____

2   c   ea   l   _____

3   m   ee   f   _____

4   w   ai   n   _____

19 **Listen and write the words.**

1 _____   2 _____   3 _____   4 _____

20 **Read aloud. Then listen and say.**

In my new jet I fly up and down, high and low. I see the clouds and the sun, the rain, and the snow. I like to be up in the sky.

21 **Write.**

Across →

1   It's rainy. It's ___ .

3   It's hot and ___ .

5   It's ___ . Let's go to the beach.

6   The _____ today is 18°.

7   18° means 18 _____ .

Down ↓

2   I can hear *KA-BOOM!* .

4   I can see ___ .

8   It's ___ . We can't go to the beach.

22 **Write.**

goes camping   go snowboarding   go water skiing
spring   summer   winter

Hi. It's ¹ _____ here, and it's really cold. I ² _____ and skiing with my friends. What's your favorite season? I don't like spring because it's rainy, but my sister loves it. She ³ _____ in the ⁴ _____ .

Hi. It's ⁵ _____ here, and it's hot. I love the beach. I ⁶ _____ _____ in the summer with my friends. It's my favorite season. I don't really like fall because it's windy.

23 Draw or stick a picture of your favorite season.

24 Write an email to your friend about your favorite season.

Hi _____. It's _____ here, and it's _____.

_____

_____

_____

_____

_____

 Are you ready for Unit 4?

4 My week

1 Match.

- do karate
- do gymnastics
- have ballet lessons
- have music lessons
- learn to cook
- learn to draw
- practice the piano
- practice the violin
- study English
- study math

2 Write.

What do you do on Saturday?

do	have	learn to
practice	study	

1 I _____ gymnastics.

2 I _____ music lessons.

3 I _____ the piano.

4 I _____ karate.

5 I _____ the violin.

6 I _____ ballet lessons.

7 I _____ math.

8 I _____ cook.

9 I _____ English.

10 I _____ draw.

3 Write.

① ② ③ ④ ⑤

| SAT 7:00 | WED 8:00 | SUN 5:00 | MON 4:00 | SAT 2:00 |

1   What does she do on Saturday?

 __She has music lessons on Saturday.__

2   What does he do on Wednesday?

 _____

3   _____ Sunday?

 _____

4   _____ Monday?

 _____

5   _____

 _____

4 Look at Activity 3 and write.

1   __She has music lessons at seven o'clock.__

2   _____

3   _____

4   _____

5   _____

5 Write.

afternoon   evening   morning   noon
quarter after eight   quarter to nine   three-thirty

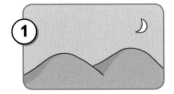 1
 2
 3
 4

_____   _____   _____   _____

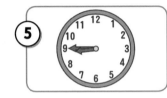 5
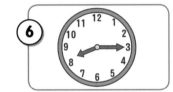 6
 7

_____   _____   _____

6  Listen and match.

 1

a

 2

b

 3

c

 4

d

 5

e

7   **Listen and draw the time. Then write.**

1 He goes swimming at _____.

2 He _____ at _____.

3 He _____ at _____.

4 _____

8 Write.

When does she learn to cook?

She learns to cook <u>in the</u>

<u>morning</u> _____.

When does he _____?

_____

_____

_____

_____

_____

_____

_____

_____

9 Number the pictures in order.

a — Then he has ballet lessons.

b — And I can swing!

c — Coco has music lessons in the afternoon.

d — That's the script!

e — He's very good.

f — I can jump...

10 Look at Activity 9 and write.

1 When does Coco have music lessons? _____

2 Does Coco practice the piano? _____

3 Does he do karate? _____

4 Can he jump and swing? _____

5 Can he do gymnastics? _____

11 Write about Coco's activities.

MON

WED

FRI

_____   _____   _____

_____   _____   _____

Try new things.

12 Number.

a Write stories. ☐

b Learn a new language. ☐

c Get a new hobby. ☐

d Learn a new instrument. ☐

e Learn self-defense. ☐

f Learn about a topic. ☐

SUMMER ACTIVITIES

① ② ③

④ Once upon a time ⑤ Bonjour! Bonjour! Learn French ⑥ All about Recycling JOIN NOW!

JOIN NOW!

13 Listen and write.

My name is Rosa. I think learning a new ¹ _____
is really fun. I want to learn the ² _____ this year.
Also, learning ³ _____ is great. I want to
learn ⁴ _____.

14 Write about new things you want to try.

My name is _____. I think _____

_____

_____

15 **Listen and write. Then number.**

① Alex: I ___walk___ to school.

② Meiling: I go to school by _____.

③ Jodie: I go to school by _____.

④ Kabir: I go to school by _____.

a ☐

b ☐

c 1

d ☐

16 **How do you and your friends go to school? Check (✓) and write.**

		by car	by bus	by bike	by boat	by train	walk
1	Me						
2							
3							

1 I _____ .

2 _____ goes _____ .

3 _____

17 **Read the words. Circle the pictures.**

glue lie pie tie

18 🎧 35 **Listen and connect the letters. Then write.**

1 c — i — ke _____

2 h a pe _____

3 d a me _____

4 sh o ve _____

19 🎧 36 **Listen and write the words.**

1 _____ 2 _____ 3 _____ 4 _____

20 🎧 37 **Read aloud. Then listen and say.**

Ha-ha-ha! The man with the tie has glue on his boots. He can't run. He is stuck with the pie in his hand.

Listen, number, and check (✓).

How are you?

22 **What does Julie do on Saturday? Write.**

Julie's Schedule	
8:00–9:00	4÷2= 8÷4= 2×2= 3×7=
9:15–10:00	
11:00–12:00	
1:30–2:00	
2:45–3:30	
4:00–4:30	

She studies math at eight o'clock.

_____

_____

_____

_____

_____

_____

_____

_____

_____

_____

23 **Write one activity for each day and when.**

SUN	MON	TUES	WED
Study math, afternoon			

THURS	FRI	SAT

24 **Look at Activity 23. Write your own questions and answers.**

1   When do you study math?

   On Sunday I study math in the afternoon.

2   _____

   On Wednesday _____.

3   _____

   On Friday _____.

4   _____

   On Saturday _____.

5   _____

   On Tuesday _____.

6   _____

   On Thursday _____.

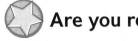 **Are you ready for Unit 5?**

5 Jobs

1 Write.

a e i o u

1 f _ r _ f _ ght _ r

2 b _ sk _ tb _ ll
   pl _ y _ r

3 b _ ll _ t
   d _ nc _ r

4 p _ l _ c _
   _ ffic _ r

5 b _ _ ld _ r

6 mov _ _ st _ r

7 _ str _ n _ _ t

8 ph _ t _ gr _ ph _ r

9 m _ ch _ n _ c

2 Write.

1 I'm an _____.

2 I'm a _____.

3 I'm a _____.

4 I'm a _____.

5 I'm a _____.

3 🎧 39 **Listen and number.**

a. ▢ 
b. ▢ 
c. ▢ 
d. ▢ 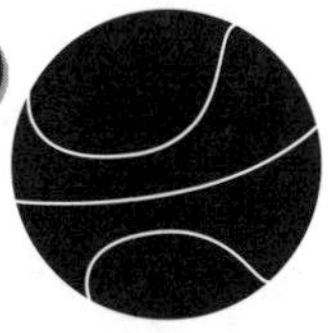
e. ▢ 
f. ▢ 
g. ▢

4 **Look at Activity 3 and write.**

1 What does she want to be? <u>She wants to be a police officer.</u>

2 What does he want to be? _____

3 _____ does _____ want to be?

_____

4 What does _____?

_____

5 _____ want to be?

_____

6 _____

_____

7 _____

_____

5 Write.

athlete   carpenter   journalist   lawyer   mechanic
model   photographer   singer

1 _____

2 _____

3 _____

4 _____

5 _____

6 _____

7 _____

8 _____

6 Unscramble and write.

1   he / want / does / to / a / be / fashion designer (✗)

Does he want to be a
fashion designer?
No, he doesn't.

2   want / be / to / lawyer / does / a / she (✔)

_____
_____
_____

3   a / do / want / be / to / you / computer programmer (✔)

_____
_____
_____

4   singer / he / want / does / to / a / be (✗)

_____
_____
_____

7 **Listen and ✓ = want or ✗ = don't want.**

1 (a)  (b)    **2** (a) COURT  (b)

3 (a)  (b)    **4** (a)  (b)

8 **Look at Activity 7 and write.**

1 He wants to be a _____. He doesn't want to be a _____.

2 She _____.

She _____.

3 _____

_____

4 _____

_____

9 **Write the questions. Then write your own answers.**

1 Do you _____? _____, I _____.

2 _____

_____

3 _____

_____

10 Write.

| computers   taking pictures   space   helping people |

1

He likes _____ .

He wants to be a _____ .

2

She _____ .

She _____ .

3

_____

_____

4

_____

_____

11 Write.

What do you want
to be, Emma?

_____

_____

12 **How much time do you spend studying? Write the number of hours.**

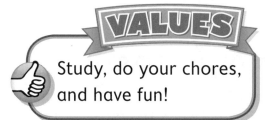

VALUES

Study, do your chores, and have fun!

① 5×2² 3(6)×2(5) 7×2 4×3	② Hello. How are you? I'm fine.	③	④

____ hours a week   ____ hours a week   ____ hours a week   ____ hours a week

13 **Do you help with chores at home? Write Y = Yes or N = No.**

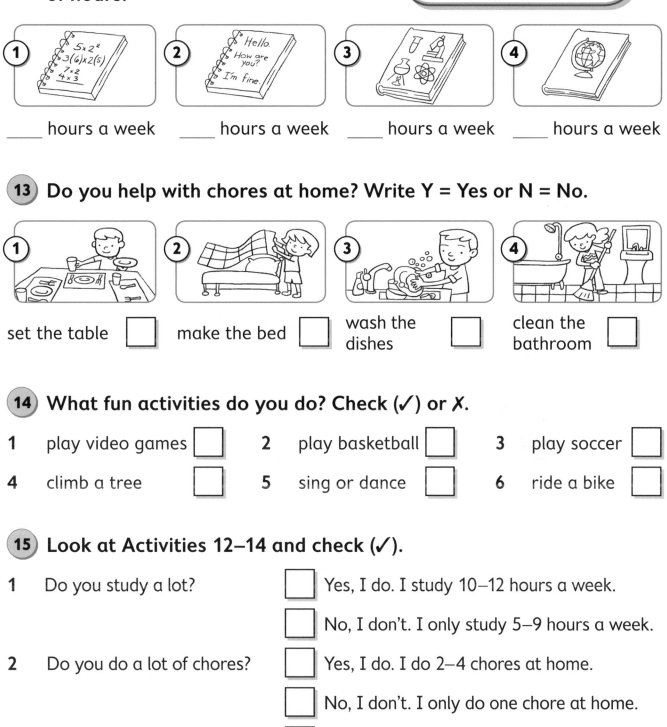

set the table ☐   make the bed ☐   wash the dishes ☐   clean the bathroom ☐

14 **What fun activities do you do? Check (✓) or X.**

1 play video games ☐   2 play basketball ☐   3 play soccer ☐

4 climb a tree ☐   5 sing or dance ☐   6 ride a bike ☐

15 **Look at Activities 12–14 and check (✓).**

1 Do you study a lot?   ☐ Yes, I do. I study 10–12 hours a week.

☐ No, I don't. I only study 5–9 hours a week.

2 Do you do a lot of chores?   ☐ Yes, I do. I do 2–4 chores at home.

☐ No, I don't. I only do one chore at home.

3 Do you play a lot?   ☐ Yes, I do. I do at least three fun activities.

☐ No, I don't. I don't do any fun activities.

16 🎧 **Listen and circle.**

1

Hello, Matthew. What do you want to be and why?

I want to be a (⚽ / 🏀) player because I love sports.

2

What do you do to make your dreams come true?

I go running at (🕐 / 🕐) in the morning. I eat only healthy food like (🥗 / 🍫). In the afternoon I practice (🏃 / 🤾) with the team.

3

What other things do you do?

I (🥋 / 🏊) on Sunday. I want to make my body strong.

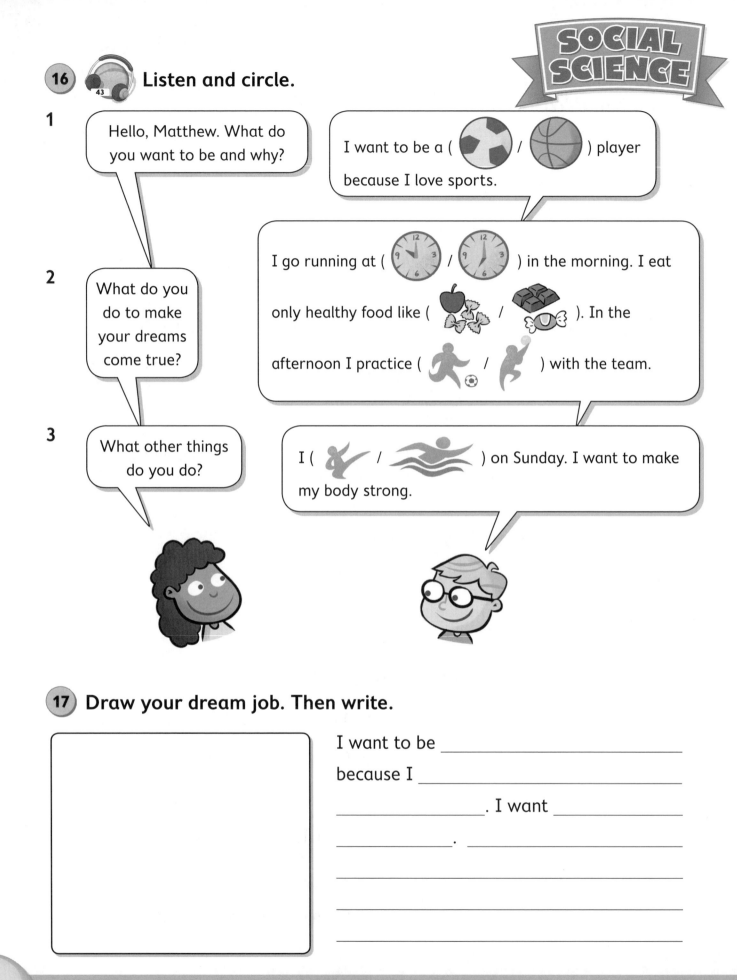

17 **Draw your dream job. Then write.**

I want to be _____

because I _____

_____. I want _____

_____. _____

_____

_____

_____

PHONICS

le   y

18 Read the words. Circle the pictures.

jungle   paddle   rainy   sunny

19 Listen and connect the letters. Then write.

1 | s | e | ll | ll | _____

2 | y | w | e | m | _____

3 | s | c | i | f | _____

4 | s | m | ar | ow | _____

20 Listen and write the words.

1 _____ 2 _____ 3 _____ 4 _____

21 Read aloud. Then listen and say.

We paddle down the river in our boat. The jungle is loud, and the sun is hot.
Look at that yellow snake! Look at that red and blue bird!

22 Write the jobs.

1 _____

2 _____

3 _____

4 _____

5 _____

6 _____

7 _____

8 _____

9 _____

10 _____

23 Listen, number, and check (✓). Then write.

a   b   COURT a   b

a   b   a   b

1 _____ Yes, he does.

2 _____ No, she doesn't.

3 What does she want to be? _____

4 What does he want to be? _____

24 **Draw and write two things you want to be or don't want to be.**

✓

I can _____ .

I like _____ .

I want to be _____ .

_____

_____

_____

✗

I don't want to be _____ .

_____

 Are you ready for Unit 6?

1 Match.

bridge   hut   mountain   river   valley   path   waterfall   cave

2 Write.

across   and   between   near   over

1 I'm swimming _____ the _____.

2 The bird is flying _____ the _____.

3 She's standing _____ the _____.

4 The _____ is _____ the lake _____ the trees.

3 Write.

1   Where's the giraffe? It's _____.

2   _____ Oliver? He's _____.

3   _____ bus? It's _____.

4   _____   _____

4 **Listen and number. Then write.**

Where are the _____?

They're _____

_____.

_____

_____

_____

_____

_____

5 Unscramble and write. Then match.

1 akle _____

2 eas _____

3 slihl _____

4 staco _____

5 stap _____

6 rowdat _____

7 orthhug _____

8 donuar _____

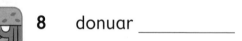

6 Read and check (✓).

1 They can't go toward the hills.

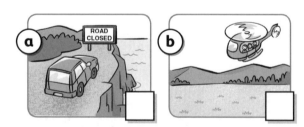

2 He can swim through the river.

3 She can't walk past the lake.

4 He can walk around the mountain.

60 Lesson 3 🎧 Sing. (See Student Book page 74.)

50

7   **Listen and number. Then write.**

a

Could she run past the lions?

_____

b

Could he swim through the lake?

_____

c

Could they go around the hills?

_____

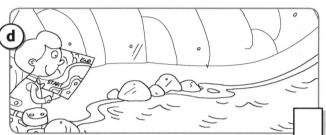

d

Could he walk toward the coast?

_____

8 **Listen and write ✓ = could or ✗ = couldn't. Then write.**

1

NORTH LAKE
10MI/16KM

2

3

4

1 We _____ go by bus, but we _____ go by plane.

2 We _____ swim _____ the lake.

3 The huts are _____ the _____ .

4 We couldn't go near the lions, but we _____ walk _____ them.

9 **Number the pictures in order.**

a Run!

b Can we look at the map?

c Here's a map.

d Thanks, Coco!

e Let's go this way.

f It's a snake!

10 **Look at Activity 9 and write.**

a Who is running over the bridge?   It's _____.

b Is Sophie looking at the map?   _____

c Does the man give a map to Sophie?   _____

d Where's Coco?   _____

e Does Oliver like maps?   _____

f Is it a rope or a snake?   _____

11 **Choose a picture from Activity 9 and write.**

I like Picture f. Sophie's with the snake. I like this picture because it's very funny.

I like Picture _____. _____

_____

12 **Write.**

VALUES

Be prepared.

6

1 He's preparing for basketball practice.

He needs:

- _____

- _____

- _____

2 She's preparing for a school trip.

She needs:

- _____

- _____

- _____

3 He's preparing for math class.

He needs:

- _____

- _____

- _____

13 **Write five things you need for each trip.**

> boots   bug spray   cap   cellphone   chocolate   compass
> first-aid kit   fishing pole   map   medicine   sandals   scarf   skis
> ski jacket   soccer ball   sunglasses   sunblock   sweater
> video game   water

A fishing trip	A skiing trip
1 _____	1 _____
2 _____	2 _____
3 _____	3 _____
4 _____	4 _____
5 _____	5 _____

14 **Write.**

> hummingbird   parrot   tapir   tarantula

1   I have a short neck.
I live near the river.
I eat bananas.
What animal am I?

_____

2   I can fly. I have a
long tail and colorful
feathers. What animal
am I?

_____

3   I can fly. I'm very
small. I like flowers.
What animal am I?

_____

4   I'm a big spider. I have
long legs. I'm scary.
What animal am I?

_____

15 **Write about your favorite rain forest animal.**

I like piranhas. They are a kind of fish. They have very sharp teeth.
They live in the Amazon River. They eat meat, fruit, and seeds. I like
them because they're scary.

I like _____

They are _____

_____

_____ I like them _____

_____

16 Read the words. Circle the pictures.

circle   circus   ice   princess

17 Listen and connect the letters. Then write.

53

1   f — e — a — p   _____

2   g — l — tt — ss   _____

3   l — l — a — g   _____

4   s — l — ee — er   _____

18 Listen and write the words.

54

1 _____   2 _____   3 _____   4 _____

19 Read aloud. Then listen and say.

55

The princess is at home, and the circus is here. It's a sunny day, and the circus is funny, but the princess isn't happy. She wants to go to the city.

PHONICS

ce   ce
ci   cir

6

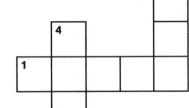

20 Write.

Across ➡

1 The boat is moving toward the  .

3 He wants to walk through the  .

5 The monkeys are in the  .

Down ⬇

2 A looks like a house.

4 A  is taller than a hill.

6 We walk on a  .

7 People use a  to get from one side to the other.

8 I want to swim in the  .

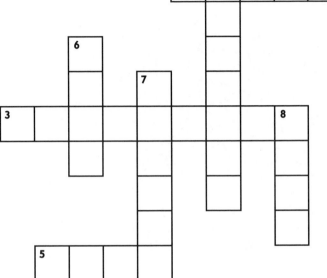

21 🎧 56 **Listen and check (✓).**

1
a
b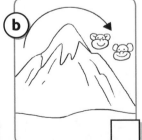

2
a
b

3
a
b

4
a
b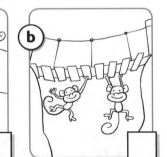

22 Draw some places on the map. Write some sentences about your map.

bridge   cave   hills   lake   mountains
path   rain forest   river   waterfall

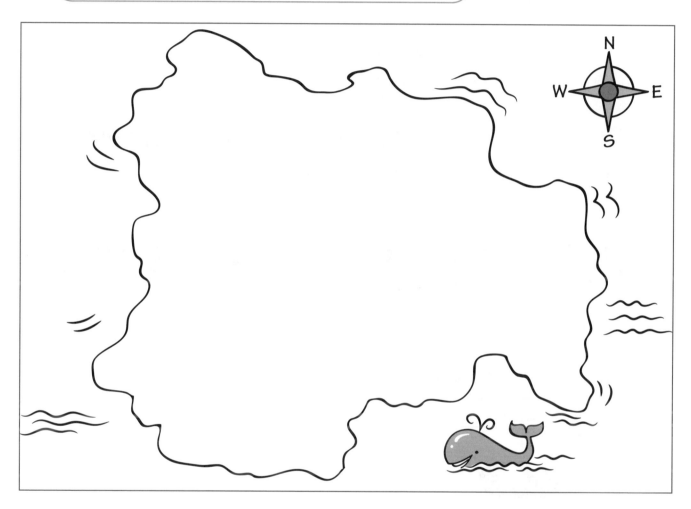

The mountains are near the lake. I could swim across the lake.

 Are you ready for Unit 7?

7 Feelings

1 Write.

> blushing crying frowning laughing shaking
> shouting smiling yawning

He's _____.

She's _____.

She's _____.

He's _____.

He's _____.

He's _____.

She's _____.

She's _____.

2 Draw the correct faces.

1 The police officer is angry.
She's shouting.

2 The builder is tired.
He's yawning.

3 The movie star is scared.
She's crying.

4 The firefighter is happy.
He's smiling.

3 **Listen and number.**

4 **Write.**

1   he / shouting / angry

Why is he <u>shouting</u>?

He's <u>shouting</u> because he's <u>angry</u>.

2   you / yawning / tired

Why are you _____?

I'm _____ because I'm _____.

3   she / smiling / happy

_____

_____

4   he / shaking / sick

_____

_____

5   you / blushing / scared

_____

_____

6   she / crying / hurt

_____

_____

7   he / frowning / bored

_____

_____

8   you / laughing / excited

_____

_____

5 Write.

embarrassed   nervous   proud   relaxed
relieved   surprised   worried

_____   _____   _____

_____   _____   _____   _____

6 Write.

1 How do you feel?

I feel _____.

2 What's the matter?

I'm _____.

3 What's the matter?

_____

4 How do you feel?

_____

7 **Listen and check (✓).**

1 sad 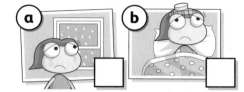

2 nervous

3 worried

4 scared

8 **Look at Activity 7 and write.**

> being sick   crocodiles   flying   rainy days
> running   singing   snakes   swimming

1 What makes you feel sad? _____ make me feel _____.

2 What makes _____?

_____ makes me feel _____.

3 What _____?

_____ makes _____.

4 _____

_____ make _____.

9  **Write.**

What's the ¹ _____? Why are you ² _____? Are you sad?

No, ³ _____. ⁴ _____ _____ because I'm worried. I failed my ⁵ _____.

10 Write.

dinosaurs   relieved   scared   worried

1   What makes Oliver feel nervous?

_____

2   What's the matter?

_____

3   How does Oliver feel?

_____

4   How does Oliver feel now?

_____

11 Write about the dinosaur.

Is it big? Does it have a long tail? Does it have sharp claws?

The dinosaur _____

_____

_____.

12 Find out about a real dinosaur. Then write.

1   Name: _____

2   Food: _____

3   Special body parts: _____

13 Number.

Help others in need.

1 Don't be embarrassed. I can help you study math at home.

2 It's OK. I can help you walk across the bridge.

3 Relax. Take it easy. You're very good at speaking.

4 Don't worry. I can help you find your mom.

a

b

c

d

14 What can you say to help? Write.

1

_____

_____

_____

_____

2

_____

_____

_____

_____

15   **Circle. Then listen to the music and number.**

It makes me feel (scared / relaxed).

I'm (crying / laughing) because it's funny.

I feel (nervous / surprised) and happy.

I'm (relieved / worried).

16 **Write the name of a song, singer, or band.**

1   What music makes you feel happy?

_____

2   What music makes you feel relaxed?

_____

3   What music makes you feel excited?

_____

4   What music makes you feel sad?

_____

17 Read the words. Circle the pictures.

| gem   gentleman   large   page |

18 Listen and connect the letters. Then write.   62

1   g   l   ee   n   _____

2   c   r   ou   n   _____

3   t   p   oo   n   _____

4   s   r   ai   d   _____

19 Listen and write the words.   63

1 _____   2 _____   3 _____   4 _____

20 Read aloud. Then listen and say.   64

The gentleman looks at the gems. There are a lot of small gems, but he likes the large gem. "How much is it?" he asks. Now he sighs. The price is too high.

21 Write.

> frowning   laughing   nervous   relaxed
> relieved   scared   shouting   smiling

She's _____ because she's

_____ .

_____

_____

_____

_____

_____

_____

22 Write.

> angry   bored   embarrassed   excited   hurt
> nervous   proud   relaxed   sad   sick   tired   worried

crying	blushing	yawning	shaking
sad			

23 Write.

My name is Mario. In this picture, I am [1] _____ because I'm excited and [2] _____. My basketball team is this year's champion. Winning a game [3] _____ feel [4] _____.

24 Draw or stick a picture of yourself. Then write.

My name is _____. In this picture, I am _____

_____

_____

_____

 Are you ready for Unit 8?

8 By the sea

1 Match.

fishing

horseback riding

kayaking

sailing

snorkeling

surfing

2 Unscramble the words. Then write.

farsorbud   file takecj   ~~ginfshi loep~~   grinid stoob   norelsk   peldad

1 Joe is ___fishing___ . He has a _fishing pole_ .

2 Oliver is _____.
He has a _____.

3 Sophie is on a _____. She loves _____.

4 Coco is _____. He's wearing _____.

5 Finley Keen is sailing, but he isn't wearing a _____.

6 Jane is kayaking, but she doesn't have a _____.

3 🎧 65 **Listen, number, and check (✓).**

4 **Write.**

1
Let's go horseback riding!

Great idea! I love _____.

2
_____

Sorry, I don't like _____.

3
_____
_____.

4
_____

Do _____ have _____ ?

Yes, I do.

5 Write.

bungee jumping   scuba diving   hang gliding   rafting   rock climbing

(1) _____ (2) _____ (3) _____

(4) _____ (5) _____

6 Write. Then listen and match.

bored with   crazy about   fond of   scared of   terrified of

 (1) _____    (a)

 (2) _____    (b)

 (3) _____   (c)

 (4) _____    (d)

 (5) _____    (e)

7 **Look at Activity 6 and write.**

1 What is she _____? She's _____.

2 What _____? _____

3 _____ _____

4 _____ _____

5 _____ _____

8 **Write.**

A: The weather is nice! Let's go
_____.

B: Sorry, I don't like sailing. I'm
_____ it.

A: Oh! Well, let's go
_____.

B: Great idea! I love _____.

A: Do you have a
_____?

B: No, I don't! Ugh!

A: What do you want to do now?

B: Let's go _____.

A: Great idea! I love _____.
I'm _____ it.

9 **Write about yourself. Then draw or stick a picture.**

What are you terrified of?	What are you _____?
I'm terrified of _____ _____.	I'm _____ _____.

10 **Number the pictures in order.**

Here's a life jacket.

a

b

My monkey!

I'm tired.

c

There's Coco.

d

Now let's make a movie.

e

I love sailing.

f

11 **Write.**

> bananas   fond of   horseback riding   knows
> making   monkey   movie star

INTERVIEW WITH
FINLEY KEEN

Finley Keen is a famous [1] _____. He's crazy about [2] _____ movies. He is also very [3] _____ sailing. His new movie is *Return to Banana Valley.*

His best friend is Coco. Coco is a very smart [4] _____. Coco wants to be a movie star like Finley Keen. He [5] _____ all the words in the new movie. Coco says, "My favorite food is [6] _____, and I'm fond of [7] _____."

12 **Write.**

1   What is Finley Keen crazy about? _____

2   What is Coco fond of? _____

13   **Listen. Then write.**

Enjoy all your activities.

> helping people   learning new things   making things
> playing sports   playing the piano   reading books

Maria

1   She enjoys _____.

2   She's excited about _____.

3   She's crazy about _____.

4   He enjoys _____.

5   He's excited about _____.

6   He's crazy about _____.

Bill

14 **Check (✓) or ✗.**

I enjoy activities that...

☐	help me exercise.	☐	start early in the morning.
☐	help me get to know my family and friends.	☐	teach languages.
☐	help me make new friends.	☐	teach math.
☐	help me protect the environment.	☐	teach science.
☐	help me relax.	☐	teach teamwork.
☐	let me help animals.	☐	teach music and the arts.
☐	let me help people.	☐	use computers.

15 **Write two activities that you enjoy or don't enjoy doing.**

✓	1	_____
	2	_____

✗	1	_____
	2	_____

16 **Write.**

| colorful   fish   hot   rain forests   sea   sea animals   white |

1   Coral reefs are called the _____ of the sea.

2   There are a lot of _____ and _____ on coral reefs.

3   Coral reefs are _____.

4   Some coral reefs die when the _____ becomes too _____.

5   Dead coral reefs are _____ in color.

17 **Write.**

| butterfly   butterfly fish   horse   lion   parrot |
| parrot fish   sea snake   seahorse   snake   starfish |

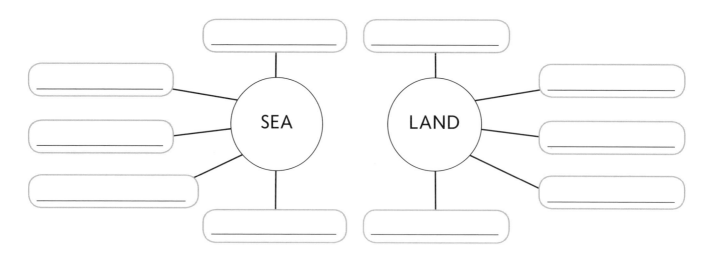

18 **Write.**

Why are most coral reefs found in hot seas?

_____

19 Read the words. Circle the pictures.

dolphin   phone   whale   whisper

20 Listen and connect the letters. Then write.
70

1 | p | i | n | y | _____

2 | b | u | nn | p | _____

3 | t | u | m | le | _____

4 | f | ai | ck | t | _____

21 Listen and write the words.
71

1 _____   2 _____   3 _____   4 _____

22 Read aloud. Then listen and say.
72

Look, the whale and the dolphin are on the phone! Here comes the shark.
The fish are whispering. What's that on his head? Oh, it's a funny hat!

23 **Write.**

A: Let's go _____! Do you
have a _____?

B: No, I don't .

A: Let's go _____! Do you
have a _____?

B: _____

A: Let's _____!
Do _____?

B: _____

A: _____!

B: Great idea. I love _____
_____.

A: _____

B: Sorry, _____
_____. I'm scared
of it.

A: I'm crazy about _____.

B: I am, too. Let's _____!

24 Write.

Hi Gerry,

I'm having a great time here in the mountains. In the morning I go 🐴

¹ _____ . I enjoy it. It makes me feel relaxed. In the

evening we go 🎣 ² _____ . But I'm 😟

³ _____ it . I don't like it very much. We are

going 🤿 ⁴ _____ on Saturday. I'm 😄

⁵ _____ it. It makes me feel proud that I can do it.

How's your vacation?

Raphael

25 Imagine you are on vacation at the beach. Write an email to a friend.

```
●○○  _____

_____
_____
_____
_____
_____
_____
_____
```

Goodbye

1 **Write.**

1   What's his name? _____

2   What _____? He likes making movies and watching TV.

3   Why _____? He's smiling because he's happy.

2 **Listen and circle.**
73

1	**a** riding a scooter	**b** skateboarding	**c** skiing
2	**a**	**b**	**c**
3	**a** Coco	**b** Sophie	**c** Oliver
4	**a** English	**b** math	**c** music
5	**a**	**b**	**c**
6	**a** Sophie	**b** Uncle James	**c** Oliver
7	**a** surprised	**b** scared	**c** relaxed
8	**a**	**b**	**c**

3 **Write.**

1

> Who is your favorite character in the story?

My favorite character is

_____ .

2

> What is your favorite chant about?

My favorite chant is about

_____ .

3

> What is your favorite song about?

_____

_____

4 **Think of your favorite movie star. Stick a picture of him/her in a scene from a movie.**

My favorite movie star is _____ .

This scene is from the movie _____ .

In this scene, he/she is _____ . I like this scene because it

makes me feel _____ .

5 **Listen and read about Willie. Then write about yourself.**

My name is Willie. I'm 10 years old. I like playing the guitar and surfing the Internet in my free time. I don't like painting or drawing. My favorite wild animal is the gorilla. Gorillas live in the rain forest, and they eat leaves and fruit.

My name is _____

_____

_____

_____

6 **Write.**

Nov 4, Sun	Nov 5, Mon	Nov 6, Tues	Nov 7, Wed	Nov 8, Thurs	Nov 9, Fri	Nov 10, Sat
28°C	19°C	20°C	28°C	25°C	19°C	19°C

1 It's Tuesday. What's the weather like today?   It's _____.

2 It's Sunday. What's the temperature today?   It's _____.

3 It's Thursday. Is it humid?   _____, it _____.

4 It's Saturday. What's the weather like today?   There's _____

_____.

5 It 's Wednesday. Is it stormy?   No, _____.

_____

7 **Listen and read about Judy. Then write about yourself.**

My name is Judy. I'm 11 years old. I study hard every day. I play basketball with my friends on Wednesday. I learn to cook with my grandmother on Saturday. When I grow up, I want to be a lawyer or journalist.

My name is _____

_____

_____

_____

8 **Listen. Then write.**

1 What makes Amy feel...

   a proud? <u>playing</u>

   b nervous? _____

2 What's Amy...

   a fond of? _____

   b bored with? _____

9 **Write.**

1 What sport can you do when it's cold and snowy? _____

2 What animal lives in rivers and eats meat? _____

3 What weather has thunder and lightning? _____

4 What time is between morning and afternoon? _____

5 What do you call a person who takes pictures? _____

6 What do you call a small wooden house? _____

7 How do people feel when they do something well? _____

8 What do you need to go kayaking? _____

Structures

Welcome

I'm **taller than** Sophie/you/him/her.
He's/She's **taller than** Sophie/you/me.
You're **taller than** Sophie/me/him/her.
My hands are **bigger**.

Unit 1 **Free time**

What do you/they **like doing?**	I/We/They **like skiing**.
What does he/she **like doing?**	He/She **likes skiing**.
I/We/They **don't like skiing**. He/She **doesn't like skiing**.	

Do you/they **like skipping?**	**Yes**, I/they **do**.
	No, I/they **don't**.
Does he/she like **skipping?**	**Yes**, he/she **does**.
	No, he/she **doesn't**.

Unit 2 **Wild animals**

Giraffes eat leaves.		
Do giraffes **eat**	leaves?	**Yes**, they **do**.
	meat?	**No**, they **don't**.

What do crabs **eat?**	**They eat** worms.
Where do crabs **live?**	**They live** in rivers.

Unit 3 The seasons

What's the weather like today?	**It's** wet.
	There's lightning and thunder.
What's the temperature today?	**It's** 25 degrees.

I/We/They **go camping** in the spring.
He/She **goes camping** in the spring.

Unit 4 My week

What	**do** you	**do** on Saturday?	**I have**	music lessons on Saturday.
	does he/she		He/She **has**	music lessons at two o'clock.

When	**do** you	have music lessons?	**I have music lessons**	in the morning.
	does he/she		He/She **has music lessons**	at 2:15.
				at quarter after two.

Unit 5 Jobs

What	**do** you	**want to be?**	**I want**	**to be**	a builder.
	does he/she		He/She **wants**		an astronaut.
I **don't**		**want to be**	a builder.		
He/She **doesn't**			an astronaut.		

Do you	**want to be** a singer?	**Yes**, I **do**.
		No, **I don't**.
Does he/she		**Yes**, he/she **does**.
		No, he/she **doesn't**.

Unit 6 In the rain forest

Where's the hut?	**It's**	**over** the mountain. **across** the bridge.
Where are the huts?	**They're**	**near** the waterfall. **between** the mountain **and** the river.

Could you **walk** around the lake?	Yes, I **could**.
	No, I **couldn't**.
I **could walk** around the lake, but I **couldn't swim** through it.	

Unit 7 Feelings

Why are you crying?	I'm crying **because** I'm sad.
Why is he/she crying?	He's/She's crying **because** he's/she's sad.

What's the matter?	**I'm** nervous.
How do you feel?	**I feel** nervous.
What makes you feel nervous?	Tests **make me feel** nervous.

Unit 8 By the sea

Let's go	snorkeling!	**Great idea!** I love snorkeling.
	kayaking!	**Sorry, I don't like** kayaking.
Do you have	a snorkel?	**Yes**, I **do**. / **No**, I **don't**.
	a paddle	

What are you crazy about**?**	**I'm** crazy about rafting.